DIGITAL
MINIMALISM

Clear Your Life of the Clutter,
Regain Your Focus and Passions.

"..Choose something else"

Lee Sebastian

Published By:

Dana Publishing
P.O. Box 1801
Mentor, OH 44060

Legal & Disclaimer

Table of Contents

Introduction

It is my hope that this guide offers you a fresh perspective with which to examine your own life, habits and perhaps make a few positive changes, starting with some cursory techniques outlined in this book. Big changes always start with small steps, sometimes very small ones.

However, if you are ambitious, you will soon uncover that the ideas and principles presented in this book can be applied to any area of your life as well. That is to say, "minimalism" may be used as a tool for enhancing your overall joy of life. As a compass leads a ship back to shore, minimalism can help lead you back to your joy, **being yourself and your passions**.

For some of you this book may be a simple reminder, or perhaps a launch pad into a different aspect of minimalism you had not heard of. And for others, this book may be your first encounter with the idea that the "things" you have spent the latter years of your life obtaining are not only incongruent with bringing you lasting joy, **but rather obstruct your connection with it.**

Some of you are already in this situation. You may just be in denial. Old things that once meant a lot to you and you had to have it, now have no meaning at all or do not bring you the pleasure, yet you hold onto to them (things or situations) simply out of programming or based on the past of who you ONCE used to be.

I personally was in this with a house and area of town I liked. I had always wanted to live in this specific area of the city, yet, I took a distant job for 2 years across country and while I was there all I could think about was going back home and buying another house in my desired neighborhood that I then came to miss severely.

But something kept telling me to broaden my horizon, look elsewhere, explore other neighborhoods, towns or even other states. Of course I ignored that prompting and did relocate back home, bought a house in the same revered neighborhood and realized after a few days that I DID not want to live there anymore at all, I outgrew it. I found another area that felt better to live in. Talk about a messed up situation. This is just one form of minimization though; I thought I had to have a house, when I could have rented a cheap apartment in a better or different place to explore, and saved a ton of cash, as well as simplifying my life by eliminating all the costs and overhead of home maintenance and repairs.

Expanding on home ownership, I now prefer to lease short term rentals so I have the freedom to up and go whenever I want to. Previously, I avoided this at all costs, being someone that prefers to have a stable "homebase", home equity, tax deductions and no shared walls with other neighbors.

However, I now value the benefits of being freed from any kind of ownership that obstructs my work or freedom. Also, I'm a single guy, so that plays a huge factor in minimizing my housing needs; as some of you reading this have a family, owning a home or long-term rental is a must.

As you probably already know, changing any habit sucks. To make any lasting change we must put ourselves in a situation of fear and dis-comfort, and confront the aspects of our lives that we find unfulfilling and "drain the swamp" so to speak. And any time you drain a swamp, you are sure to drudge up a LOT of crap, and in this case, **inner resistance**.

To bring about change will force you to create new habits, step out of your comfort zone and it **will** HURT. But I invite you to embrace these negative feelings, as these are merely proof that you are on the right track to **real**, lasting change.

As the author of this book, my goal is not to convince you to suddenly renounce your possessions and move to the hills of Italy to herd sheep. My intention with this book is to help you bring YOU back into your life. I often use the words "**you**" and "**joy**" interchangeably, and this is because I view them as one in the same. By decluttering your life, you will find more of you, and where there is you, there is always joy.

May this book bring you both ideas and inspiration for change, and the confidence to follow through with your endeavors, however big or small they may be.

Chapter 1: Forms of Minimalism

Since there are no official distinctions or types of minimalism, everyone has to find out for themselves what suits them and how they want to live. There are forms of minimalism that have prevailed more and those that have prevailed less. The goal of a minimalist life is to lead a conscious life with which you can better identify. That's why I'm advising you to find your personal, proper, minimalist lifestyle. For some, it is quite enough to question and change their own behaviour in certain situations. Others want to make a complete change and change their lives by 180 degrees. What is the right thing for you and whether minimalism is the right thing at all, you will have to decide for yourself.

The Essentialist

As you can see from the name, this minimalist type is concerned with the essentials. In practice, this can mean that you own as few things as possible, but very high-quality ones. Surplus of such things is only ballast and so it is not about saving money, but to have the right thing that lasts longer and gives pleasure. "Quality before quantity" is the motto of this minimalist lifestyle. That doesn't mean that you should buy less but more expensive things. Ultimately, it is about dealing better and more intensively with the goods you consume.

The Strict

For this minimalist type, the main thing is to set <u>oneself strict guidelines and implement them strictly.</u> He/she wants to prove something, so to speak, and act with discipline. A default could be, for example, that you turn to exactly 100 things. If you have 110 things, 10 are sorted out. You only keep the 100 most important things. We also give this minimalist type a lot of time for intensive examination of the things one wants to possess. Strict guidelines mean that the consumption of various goods must be well thought out.

The Naturalist

This minimalist lifestyle is someone who clearly questions, restricts and defines his field of action. As already mentioned, minimalism is often about doing the environment a favor. If one looks at the general way of life of people, it is most urgently necessary that people change their way of thinking. Because if we don't live minimalistically, we're contributing to global warming.

Global warming is continuing to advance and the consequences are real. One could say that people behave as if they had inherited the earth from their ancestors. To put this into practice, naturalists are reducing their ecological status. For example, they use organic or Fairtrade products. Driving a car, for example, is avoided because the exhaust gases are harmful to the environment. The bicycle becomes the most important means of transport for naturalists. The naturalists also take things such as waste and refuse separation very seriously.

The Spiritual

This type focuses most of the attention and minimalism on themselves by getting to know and appreciate their inner attributes. The mind plays an important role for this type, as does self-observance. After all, the mind is the plant of its own perception, which wants to be permanently watered. We are on a never-ending journey in which we get to know ourselves. We get to know others and get to know many new things. As you know, you never stop learning. Since many people are already attracted to this method and want to experience it, it shows that the general trend for mindfulness exercise is increasing. Trends such as yoga exercises are also on the rise, as the inner center can be easily found and balanced.

The Adventurer

Just grab a backpack and go out into the big, wide world. Who hadn't thought of doing something like this before? This is precisely the lifestyle of the adventurer.. You only need a little money, but a lot of openness and open-mindedness to find your way out there. You can do freelance work to make income while adventuring, because to really get far you obviously have to come up with mney here and there.

You have to be able to think and plan. This type of minimalism goes so far that even the existence of a home-base is released. Home can just be the world, so to speak. The consumption and possession of various goods is only needed for survival. It takes courage to embrace such a big lifestyle. You also need the right character traits, such as a thirst for adventure, spontaneity and curiosity, risk and unknowns in order to constantly live in new adventures and challenges, to get to know new people and new places. However, I think that once you have decided on such a journey, you will return one day with unforgettable memories.

Maybe you feel attracted to multiple forms of minimalism. This is also not about filtering and categorizing. The forms and types of minimalist lifestyles I have presented to you are for orientation and inspiration only. In the end, it's all about finding the right level of minimalism for yourself without restricting your zest for life. After all, it is not a matter of doing without, but of living according to the motto "less is more" in a meaningful and individually correct way. In the beginning it seems to be a bit much for a newcomer, but once you've got the start behind you, the rest will take care of itself.

Chapter 2: Getting Started

With technology constantly evolving, most of our time is spent looking at screens. When we are working, we spend it on a computer. Even when taking a break, we simply grab the phone, play video games, browse, or chat.

One of the problems created by these habits is the amount of digital clutter we end up with. Clutter doesn't just include the files on our desktop or the bookmarks on the browser, but also the accounts managed on social media, the emails clogging up our inbox, apps we installed but forgot about, etc.

Clutter eventually slows down the computer and takes away space we could have used to store important data. All this mess is often a huge productivity-killer without us even realizing.

Think about it. You might be one of those people who save everything to the desktop when in a rush, thinking you would sort it out later. But what happens is that you just keep adding until it becomes more difficult to find something until you eventually start throwing the files into a random folder instead. Scrolling through these endless folders to find the thing you want becomes overwhelming and breaks focus.

How did we reach this point?

Before technology took over, families used to sit at a table for dinner and share the events of their day while they ate. Children would do homework with a pencil and paper using a pile of hard copy books to look up facts while their parents read the news on a printed newspaper or listen to the radio. For fun, families would take a walk to the park, play board games, or share stories. Communication outside the house consisted of writing letters, making phone calls, or meeting somewhere.

But now we simply watch TV while eating, turn to Google for answers, play games on computers, chat by text, email, browse, YouTube, Facebook, etc. This is how drastically technology changed the way we do work, spend time, and entertain ourselves.

In a short time, the Internet has moved from an uncommon tool to our primary way of life.

Although the time spent online continues to increase, research state that people actually want to decrease that time. But unfortunately, their obsession with technology doesn't allow them to disconnect. Digital devices are everywhere and always within reach, even in the bed. This creates anxiety and a feeling of being lost if the device is not in our hands. Just like an addiction, we became slaves to technology and would require some effort to break free.

Technology might be convenient, but it is important to recognize that we need balance in our lives. Excessive use can lead to health dangers such as eye strain, muscle tension, obesity, carpal tunnel syndrome, sleep disorders, and even death. Realizing that you have a problem is the first step to free your mind from the clutter created by digital devices.

How do you know if you have a clutter problem?

Ask yourself the following questions to get an idea of your situation:

- Do you mostly turn to the search tool in order to find things?

- Do you get overwhelmed when going through your bookmark list?

- Do you collect too many emails during the years and just let them pile up in your inbox?

- Do you have many duplicate photos?

- Is your storage device over 75 percent full?

- Do you have many applications you never use?

- In what state is your desktop?

- Does your computer run slow, freeze up or have security issues?

- Do you know most of the "friends" you have on social media?

- How do you feel when you work on your digital devices?

If you answered yes to most of these questions, then you definitely should not ignore it any longer.

Unlike physical clutter in your home, digital clutter can go by unnoticed for years. Once you finally tackle the problem, you would be surprised how much it can improve your life.

Advantages of Digital Declutter

Here are the prime reasons to inspire you to declutter:

1. Declutter speeds up digital devices

No digital device lasts forever, but you can prolong its average lifespan. All the unnecessary files and programs cause stress on the system and will run much faster and smoother once you clear them out.

2. It reinforces computer security

Unused and outdated software is a huge security risk for your devices. Eliminating these programs removes access for a potential hacker.

3. Declutter boosts productivity

Without distractions to interrupt tasks, you will automatically be more productive. When every item is in its rightful place, you won't have to break focus in order to find it first.

4. It improves concentration

It's not easy to focus when your attention is always required by something else. Without all those incoming emails, application notifications, icons, and tabs, you can stay fully concentrated for longer.

5. Declutter reduces stress

Clutter negatively impact peace of mind. Most people want an organized environment. If an area is messy, it frustrates the mind because of obstacles preventing it from completing tasks smoothly. Once those obstacles are out of the way, the reduced strain calms the mind.

6. It builds confidence and makes you more disciplined

Having a clean digital environment will make you feel fantastic and motivated. Once you see how well organized your devices are after a declutter routine, you will be more disciplined in order to keep it that way so that your hard work wasn't for nothing.

7. Declutter increases energy and invites creativity

Creativity requires us to be in the best mindset. Clutter clouds the mind and drags us down while decluttering brings clarity and gives us an emotional boost. Without energy it would be impossible to accomplish anything, physically or emotionally.

8. It improves real-world interactions

The more time you must spend online, the less you have for the real world. An organized device means spending less time finding what you need so that you can finish work faster and spend some quality time with people you love.

9. It helps to locate lost items

You'd be surprised how many things you'll find that you thought were long gone, especially if you have had the computer or device for years. It might be something important or just a photo with sentimental value.

10. Declutter gives a fresh start

Freeing up space and organizing your devices give you the chance to devote your attention to new, exciting things. Just as an uncluttered home breathes pure energy into a room, an uncluttered device results in a more productive experience. It creates direction and revives your ability to process information.

Clutter Types and Where to Start

Common types of digital clutter:

When dealing with clutter, there are a few things to watch out for, here's how to identify what is important and what can be eliminated.

Hopeful Clutter:

These are the type of files people save, *hoping* to use them someday. It includes unread e-books, blog posts, emails, bookmarks, and downloads. The list only grows longer and longer over time, making it almost impossible to get back to them. But because of the desire to improve ourselves, we cling to this list, which only manages to frustrate us instead.

Instead of hoping for a future where we will be able to use these items, we should live in the present and do things that make us happy.

Doubtful Clutter:

These are the type of clutter you have stored over the last few years and just don't want to let go, because what if you need them in the future?

These refer to old projects from a job you left years ago, interesting articles you have collected, scanned receipts, etc.

We all worry that an item might be important after it's gone and that's why we should rather hang on to it. But have you ever really needed or used any of those items you have collected over the years? Most likely, they can just be scrapped as another pile of digital clutter.

Bargain Clutter:

Who doesn't like free or bargain items. Newsletters that offer free downloads upon signing up, coupon websites, and email notifications of a huge sale, are often the culprits here. They make it feel like the most incredible offer ever and you end up falling for it every time. The item then ends up sitting on your device unused, either because you never had the time for them, or because you completely forgot about them.

We think we save money by going for these offers and that we might need it at some point, but that is rarely the case.

Useless Clutter:

These are the type of clutter you once thought was worth keeping but are now outdated and unnecessary. But because it is too much effort and you have better things to do with your time, you just leave it on the device to take up space. These can refer to old software, emails, photos, documents, etc. It might not be how you want to spend your time, but don't leave the items until it becomes a problem.

"Homeless" Clutter:

This is the type of clutter that doesn't really have a place on your device. So, you let it sit in a temporary folder until you can figure out where to put it, but often ends up forgotten. They can include any type of file such as downloads, documents, photos, software, screenshots, etc.

It is hard to pinpoint their exact value. The file might belong under hopeful clutter and can also be important information. But if you can't find the file when you need it, its value doesn't really matter.

Sentimental Clutter:

These are the files with emotional attachments and are one of the hardest things to let go of. Either because of a memory related to the item or because you don't want to offend the person if you delete it. These often include memorable photos, old emails from family, friends, or someone romantic, projects you completed, etc.

But it is difficult to be sentimental when you can't even

remember where the sentiment is stored. With the growing list of sentimental items, you don't have time to go through these past reminders anyway and ends up as yet another thing that just tempts you away from the real world.

Actions to take when starting your first declutter attempt:

Pick a date and time

Set a time when you know you will have some free time so that it doesn't conflict with other obligations. Preferably, the time shouldn't change much from day to day otherwise you won't be able to build consistency.

Choose a quiet place

Decluttering would be impossible if you are constantly interrupted. So, before you begin, make sure that people won't barge in and ruin your plans.

Create your perfect atmosphere

Some people work best in a quiet environment, while others prefer music or the noise of nature. Choose the one that works best for you, as long as you make it consistent. Consistency is the key to creating a trigger in your mind to form a habit.

Get rid of all distractions

Turn off all notifications and close excessive tabs. Don't allow temptations to distract you during the duration of your decluttering time.

Choose where you want to start

It is best to start with the device that you use the most. But the choice is up to you, as long as you make a start somewhere.

Try to make fast decisions

You will be faced with many items you wouldn't know how to handle. To avoid being stuck with an endless supply of questions, make your decisions quick. If it's something you can easily get again and don't use regularly, don't hesitate to delete.

Do 10 minutes at a time

Sticking to a 10-minute routine will make it easier to start and achieve your goal. Don't be tempted to do too much at once, otherwise you will just burn yourself out and waste time.

Chapter 3: What is Digital Detox?

There are a few ways to treat technology addiction. One way is to seek counseling from a therapist. This can be done in a private or group setting.

Another option is rehab. This approach works in the same was as drug or alcohol rehab. You visit a treatment center for a specific period of time - for example, two weeks - during which your access to technology is restricted. Some clinics offer outpatient programs, but as with outpatient drug and alcohol rehab, there's a high rate of relapse.

The third approach is self-treatment. Rather than visiting a therapist or signing yourself into a rehab facility, you take the reins in breaking your addiction. You're in control.

Here, we're talking about doing a personal digital detox.

The advantages of self-treatment are twofold. First, it's less expensive than therapy or enrollment into a rehab facility. Second, it poses less disruption to your current lifestyle.

If you're like me, those two advantages seal the deal.

Below, I'll explain what a digital detox is, and present the reasons to do one. If you're addicted to text messaging, video games, social media, news headlines, or YouTube, you're about to discover one of the best remedies.

Digital Detox Explained

A digital detox involves stepping away from all of your gadgets. This includes your phone, tablet, and laptop.

There are a number of challenges to traveling this path. For example, how do you unplug completely if your job requires you to use a computer? Additionally, how can you keep in touch with people without texts, emails, and phone calls?

And what about withdrawal symptoms?

A digital detox is like a drug detox. Your brain craves the dopamine rush that results from your compulsive behavior. Once you cut off your access to technology, you'll feel the pangs of withdrawal.

I'll address these and other challenges in the following chapters. The important thing to remember is that breaking your addiction requires the removal of your phone and other tech-related tools. Weaning yourself is not enough if you hope to control your dependency. You need to sever the connection, at least temporarily.

Think of it this way: if you were addicted to cocaine, you wouldn't try to break your addiction by gradually reducing the number of lines you do each night. That strategy is guaranteed to fail. Instead, you'd check yourself into a clinic and undergo a complete detox, one with no access to cocaine.

That's how you need to approach your addiction to technology. If you want to break the habit, stop feeling overwhelmed, and regain control of your focus and productivity, you need to do a complete digital detox.

You'll probably need motivation. I strongly encourage you to write down the many ways your life will improve after you break your technology addiction. Review the list whenever you experience signs of withdrawal.

The Reasons You're Addicted To Technology

We use technology to increase our productivity, gain knowledge and insight, and make personal connections on a scale that would be impossible without it. Our phones and other devices enrich our lives in myriad ways.

The problem is, continued use makes us increasingly dependent on them. The more we use our phones, tablets, and laptops for non-work activities - for example, surfing Facebook and Pinterest or playing games - the greater becomes our dependency on them.

That's the road to addiction.

In the previous chapter, we talked about a variety of factors that make you more susceptible to developing an obsession with technology. This chapter will explore the reasons you may be hooked on it. Once you recognize the root causes of your addiction, you'll find it easier to overcome it via a digital detox.

Information Overload

Thirty years ago, information came at us in the form of a stream. We had newspapers, magazines, and a handful of television programs. We visited the library if we needed to research topics.

It was manageable.

Today, information comes at us in the form of a flood. A ridiculous amount arrives through our phones, computers, and hundreds of cable TV channels every day. We increase the load by setting up Google Alerts, subscribing to email newsletters, bookmarking dozens of websites and blogs, and spending hours on social media.

And of course, our Kindles are filled with hundreds, even thousands, of books yet to be read.

We're drowning in information. We're being overwhelmed by a continuous torrent of content.

This keeps us addicted to technology. We struggle to keep our heads above water while at the same time craving more information and entertainment.

Dopamine Rush

The release of dopamine in our brains is the one constant behind all addictions. Studies have shown that playing video games triggers its release. Spending time on Facebook, reading text messages, and searching Google does, too. You experience the same effect when you inhale nicotine, drink caffeine, and take hits of cocaine (or so studies show).

This little neurotransmitter is one of the biggest reasons we become addicted to our drugs of choice, whether we're talking about illicit narcotics or our phones.

Dopamine fills us with a sensation of pleasure. That's a hard thing to turn your back on. Once you experience the sensation, you want to experience it again and again.

Our phones make doing so simple. We receive a text from a friend and feel a small rush. We notice new emails in our inboxes and feel a small rush. We see new activity on Facebook and Twitter, and feel a small rush.

That's dopamine.

It's one of the reasons you may be addicted to your phone, video games, news headlines, and social media. Just as surely as the cocaine addict is always on the lookout for his next hit, the technology addict is always looking for her next fix - whatever will trigger the small dopamine rush her brain craves will suffice.

Anonymity

On blogs, forums, and social media, anonymity equates to safety. We can interact with people, argue with them, ridicule them, and express unpopular ideas, comforted by the thought that no one truly knows who we are.

They don't know our names. They don't know where we live.

It's unsurprising people are willing to say things online they would never say in the physical presence of others. Their anonymity protects them.

Being anonymous also encourages voyeurism. We go online to watch others - some call it stalking - and sate our curiosity about them. What are they doing? Who are they talking to? What are they saying, and about whom are they saying it?

The activity, a combination of people-watching and eavesdropping, can easily become addictive. For the person who already struggles with an obsession with technology, it's likely to feed her habit and reinforce her dependency.

Fear of Missing Out

The fear of missing out is a powerful motivator. In fact, many companies use it as a sales technique. For example, you've probably seen advertisements claiming that only a limited number of a certain product are available at the advertised price. It's an effective marketing tactic because it provokes our fear of missing out on a rewarding experience (i.e. getting a great deal).

Think about that in the context of reading texts, listening to voice-mails, checking email, visiting Facebook, and reading the latest news headlines. Our compulsion to do these things is driven by the same apprehension. We don't want to miss something.

You've no doubt seen people read - or worse, respond to - texts while driving. You've seen people check their email while sitting in restaurants and movie theaters. They're not addressing emergencies. They're just fearful of missing out.

As I mentioned earlier, the more often we behave in a specific manner - for example, reaching for our phones to read texts the instant they arrive - the more likely the behavior will become a habit. Repetition reinforces the behavioral pattern. Once the behavior becomes a habit, repeated application can turn it into a compulsion. And that's one step away from it becoming a full-blown addiction.

Gateway of Good Intentions

No one plans to become addicted to their smartphones, tablets, and other devices. We use technology with the intention to make our lives better.

For example, we use spreadsheets at our workplaces to meet our job responsibilities. We set up **Google Alerts** to save us time on research. We go online to book hotels and airline flights for family vacations.

In other words, technology itself isn't the problem. On the contrary, our phones, computers, and the internet make us more productive and effective. They improve our lives in countless ways.

But counterintuitively, our good intentions can set the stage for the onset of addiction. Individuals, who routinely use technology to save time, get things done, or do their jobs may gradually develop an obsession.

Those who have an obsessive personality or are easily distracted are the most vulnerable. The more they use their phones and other tools, the more they reinforce their compulsive behaviors.

For example, checking email becomes less about keeping on top of work-related projects and more about the excitement (and dopamine rush) triggered by the activity.

Societal Expectations

Thirty years ago, people looked curiously - even suspiciously - at those who carried cellphones. The devices were an oddity. And if you owned a laptop, you were considered among the high-tech elite!

Things have changed.

Technology has become a large part of our daily experience. Whether we're at the office, relaxing at home, or on vacation, we're expected to carry our phones and other devices with us. An undercurrent of societal pressure makes us feel naked without them.

This dynamic has made it nearly impossible to function

without our gadgets. That's problematic for those who struggle with a phone addiction, internet addiction, or compulsive behavior related to anything involving technology.

We feel pressured to respond to texts and emails the moment we receive them. We feel pressured to answer our phones when people call us. We feel pressured to keep up on whatever is happening on social media.

Each time we act on our impulses, we reinforce our compulsive behaviors and feed our addiction.

The Tech Industry Encourages Compulsive Behavior

I've likened technology addiction to drug addiction. They share a number of similarities. As noted, engaging in either activity triggers the release of dopamine, a key part of the brain's reward system. That creates and sustains the addiction.

But an addiction to technology is different than an addiction to drugs in at least one important way. And it's one the tech industry relies on to encourage compulsive behavior in consumers.

The fancy term for it is "intermittent reinforcement."

It's the practice of using sporadic rewards to reinforce a particular behavior. The term springs from research conducted by psychologist and behaviorist B.F. Skinner in the 1950s.

Here's how it works in the context of checking Facebook. Each time you visit Facebook, you hope to discover something new and interesting. Maybe a friend has posted new photos of her dog. Perhaps your sibling has posted a funny video or a link to an entertaining article.

There's no guarantee you'll find new content that interests you every time you log onto Facebook. That is, there's no guarantee that visiting the site will produce a reward. But if it does so, you'll experience the familiar dopamine rush with its attendant positive feelings.

That's "intermittent reinforcement" at work. According to Skinner, it ensures you'll keep coming back.

Technology companies know this. They use "intermittent reinforcement" as a tactic to encourage your compulsiveness. That includes visiting social media sites, checking your email, reading texts, searching Google, and watching YouTube videos. Each of these platforms are designed to keep you engaged with rewards delivered at irregular intervals.

The same forces are at play when you sit down in front of a slot machine. You don't win with every pull of the lever. You win intermittently. The sporadic rewards keep you in your seat, hoping the replicate the experience.

No Plan To Control The Obsession

The seeds of addiction are planted early. The New York Times reported in 2010 that kids between 8 and 18 years of age spend seven and a half hours a day consuming various forms of media. How? With their phones, tablets, computers, and other devices.

That was several years ago. Technology is playing an even greater role in our lives today. Indeed, CNN reported in late 2015 that teens now spend **9 hours a day** watching videos, listening to music, and playing video games. Some of them visit sites like Facebook and Instagram more than 100 times each day.

As one expert noted, "the sheer volume of media technology that kids are exposed to on a daily basis is mind-boggling."

Adults have even more exposure. According to a 2014 Nielsen report, **U.S. adults spend 11 hours a day consuming media.**

Here's the troubling part: there's rarely a plan, or even an intent, to control this obsession. Parents seldom warn their kids that constant use of phones and other gadgets will reinforce compulsive behaviors and eventually lead to addiction. Indeed, few of us adults take steps to short-circuit that process in our own lives.

Instead, we surrender to the siren call of technology. Rather than limiting our exposure, we surround ourselves with gadgets that continuously feed our obsession.

Every addiction, whether to alcohol, drugs, or gambling, carries consequences. An addiction to technology is no exception. In the next chapter, we'll take a quick look at how your tech addiction is negatively impacting your life.

Chapter 4: How Technology Addiction Negatively Impacts Your Life

Most addicts realize their addictions will harm them in the long run. But in the short run, the objects of their obsessions, from drugs and shopping to gambling and chocolate, bring them such a rush that it's difficult to set them aside. Moreover, the immediate consequences of feeding the addiction seem minimal given the immediate payoff.

Technology addiction, like all types of addictions, poses numerous potential consequences. The consequences might seem relatively harmless in the short run, but will introduce major problems in the long run.

Below, we'll address these problems in detail. That way, you'll be aware of the true cost of your obsession when it comes to using your phone, the internet, and other tech-related tools.

Sleeping Problems

In 2014, **Sleep Review: The Journal For Sleep Specialists** reported that cell phone addicts are among the most sleep-deprived individuals. Research has pointed to several possible factors.

First, addicts tend to take their phones to bed with them. This disrupts their circadian systems, or body clocks. Their bodies are consequently less able to regulate when they should sleep and awaken.

Second, the fear of missing out keeps people glued to their phones and laptops long after they should have gone to bed. Because most people need to get up early in the morning, the habit cuts into their sleep.

Third, the type of light emitted by our gadgets' screens - called "blue light" - is believed to play a role. Experts claim blue light tells our brains it's not yet time to go to sleep. Staring at our phones and tablets before going to bed is bound to keep us awake.

Insufficient sleep produces swift, negative side effects. If you're not getting enough sleep, you'll be irritable, more prone to making mistakes, and less able to concentrate. Worse, over time, you'll become more vulnerable to a range of serious health issues.

Increased Restlessness

Have you ever found it difficult to relax because you're waiting to receive an important phone call or email? Have you had difficulty focusing on your work because you're waiting for a friend to respond to your text?

You feel restless.

Restlessness can manifest in a variety of ways. For example, you may be unable to sit still. You might suffer a low level of anxiety. You may be so preoccupied with the object of your attention - e.g. a forthcoming email or text - that you're powerless to focus on anything else, no matter the priority.

Compulsive use of your phone, the internet, and other tech-related tools leads to increased restlessness. Technology allows us to live our lives at a faster pace than ever before. We can obtain information faster. We can connect with, and respond to, friends and family members faster. We can feed our insatiable appetite for new content (videos, blogs, social media posts, etc.) with the click of a button.

This can be an advantage in certain circumstances. For example, if we're trying to meet a tight deadline, and need information to move a project forward, having the ability to obtain that information quickly is valuable.

But this faculty can just as easily become a liability. With every imaginable form of information and every personal connection literally at our fingertips, it's easy to form unrealistic expectations. We expect instant gratification.

When those expectations prove to be false - for example, we're forced to wait for a friend or client to respond to an email - we become restless.

Life is full of such inconveniences. They require patience. Being in a state of constant restlessness is no way to live your life.

Anxiety And Stress

Are you feeling stressed, but unable to identify the reasons? Do you feel anxious despite meeting your personal goals and work-related responsibilities?

It's not a mystery if you spend a considerable amount of time on your phone or the internet. Anxiety and stress are common companions of technology addiction. Studies show that overexposure to the internet can influence your emotional state. It can lead to loneliness and depression, both of which increase your stress levels.

The anxiety and stress occur due to several reasons. Technology addiction disrupts the relationships you share with friends and family members; it causes you to neglect your job responsibilities; it leads to social isolation; and it can eventually open the door to financial problems.

We also noted earlier that an obsession with your phone or the internet can negatively affect your sleep. That too can increase your stress levels. Lack of sleep, especially when sustained over an extended period, triggers the release of cortisol, a stress hormone.

The more stress and anxiety you feel, the less effective you'll be in anything you attempt. You'll be less present when spending time with your family. You'll be less able to concentrate at work. You'll be more irritable and struggle more with distractions. Worse, you'll expose yourself to a long list of health issues, including diabetes, heart disease, high blood pressure, as well as problems with digestion, memory, and sexual function.

A digital detox will help to eliminate the stress you're feeling so you can regain control of your life.

Inability To Focus

We take the ability to focus for granted. We assume we can do it whenever we need to. The reality is that our compulsive behaviors toward technology erode that ability. The more time we spend with our phones and other gadgets, the less we're able to concentrate on whatever task we're trying to complete.

Our thoughts become fragmented. Our attention is quickly lost to distractions. We start to multitask, which further taxes our unfocused brains. Every piece of outside stimuli attracts our notice.

How does this loss of focus impact you? There are several side effects. You become forgetful and miss appointments and deadlines. You become a less engaged - and less engaging - conversationalist. Your situational awareness suffers. You become more impulsive and prone to outbursts. You require more time than necessary to complete projects and activities.

In short, an inability to focus stemming from an addiction to technology can have long-ranging negative impacts on your life.

There are numerous strategies for improving your focus. One is to unplug. If you're struggling with an internet addiction, a phone addiction, or any other tech-related obsession, you need a digital detox.

Inability To Retain Information

Short-term memory loss is often seen in those who struggle with internet addiction. Scientists aren't certain of the reasons, but suspect they might be related to changes in the brain's structure.

In 2011, researchers in China studied the effects of internet addiction on brain gray matter. They found evidence that overexposure to the internet resulted in "multiple structural changes in the brain." They went on to note that "structural abnormalities in the internal capsule could consequently interfere with the cognitive function and impair executive and memory functions." (Their findings were published in the journal PLoS ONE.)

It's tempting to dismiss signs of memory loss as inconsequential. For example, we assign little significance to our inability to remember where we put our car keys. But unless the forgetful individual takes steps to prevent further memory erosion, "inconsequential" signs can introduce troubling circumstances down the road. Loss of short-term memory may gradually influence his emotions, motor function, reflexes, and ability to communicate.

Scientists continue to study how internet addiction affects the brain's numerous processes, including short-term memory storage. If you struggle to remember things and have a compulsion to go online, now is a good time to curb the habit.

Greater Susceptibility To Distractions

By now, it shouldn't surprise you that an addiction to your phone or the internet will make you more vulnerable to distractions. The worst part is that the effect is insidious, and thus often escapes notice.

It happens to everyone. In 2015, Pew Research released its findings concerning smartphone use in the U.S. Nearly 60% of survey respondents reported feeling regularly "distracted" as a direct result of their phones.

It's reasonable to assume the actual figure is higher. After all, many people are disinclined to admit any type of shortcoming. Moreover, some phone addicts may be unaware of the problem.

Our phones can also present the seductive mirage of increased productivity. Many of the survey respondents noted that using their phones made them **feel** as if they were more productive despite increased distractions.

Distractions are the enemy of productivity. Interruptions destroy your momentum, increasing the time it takes you to get something done. Whether the interruption comes in the form of a coworker with a question or an urge to check Facebook, it causes your brain to stumble. Each time this happens, your brain needs up to 20 minutes to get itself back on track.

With that in mind, imagine the daily experience of a technology addict. She's constantly on her phone or surfing the internet. Every few minutes, she checks for new emails and texts, plays games, logs into social media, reads the latest news, or visits her favorite online forums.

Can you imagine how difficult it would be for her to focus on her work or the person she's with? The constant distractions would make doing so impossible.

Being distracted by your phone also poses other issues. For example, it impairs interpersonal bonding. Many people consider it rude to acknowledge texts, emails, and phone calls in their company. Additionally, using your phone while driving can have catastrophic results.

If you're addicted to your phone, you probably don't consider the constant distractions to be a problem. At least, not yet. That perspective will change once you go through a digital detox. You'll notice a dramatic difference in your level of awareness in the absence of your gadgets.

Reduced Productivity

The more often you're distracted, the less productive you'll be. Given that a phone obsession or internet addiction opens the door to an endless string of distractions, your productivity is sure to decline.

Many people mistakenly assume their gadgets make them more productive. The perception is understandable. After all, they can check their email, manage their schedules, and respond to questions instantly via text.

But the perception is oftentimes an illusion. More often than not, our phones and other devices serve as obstacles to our attempts to get things done.

The economist Robert Solow addressed this notion in 1987 when he noted "**You see the computer age everywhere but in the productivity statistics.**" Although the advent of smartphones, tablets, and wi-fi internet access was still several years away, Solow's comment was insightful. Even prescient.

The truth is, many of us waste a considerable amount of time online each day. We're constantly distracted, with our attention pulled in a thousand directions. The result is that we're regularly unable to get as much done as we hope.

Think about how you currently use the internet. You might spend an hour each day reading and replying to emails. You may spend an hour each morning reading news headlines and watching YouTube videos. Perhaps you spend a few hours in the afternoons playing online games, surfing social media sites, and reading your favorite blogs. Maybe your evenings are spent shopping or gambling online.

These activities can take up a considerable portion of your day. That leaves you with significantly less time to complete important tasks and projects.

Over the past 10 years, there has been a surge of productivity apps you can download to your phone and browser. These apps are seductive because they hold the promise of increased productivity. But the developers rarely mention that becoming more productive is more a matter of developing good habits than simply downloading the latest apps.

If you're currently struggling to finish projects on time, consider how much time you spend on the internet and your phone. It's possible you've developed an obsession. If that's the case, your compulsive behaviors are almost certainly hampering your productivity.

Strained Relationships

Technology addiction can take a dramatic toll on the relationships you share with the people in your life. Consider the phone addict who checks her phone every couple of minutes. She's unable to carry on a meaningful conversation due to the constant interruptions. Understandably, the person she's with is likely to think of her behavior as rude.

Consider the internet addict who can't pull himself away from his computer. He's obsessed to the point that he'd rather stay online than retire to bed with his spouse.

Technology addiction impairs relationships in numerous ways. Some are less than obvious.

For example, it hampers the intimacy shared between spouses. An endless string of text messages, email notifications, and event reminders creates an ever-present distraction that makes communication and intimacy difficult, if not impossible.

It causes the person spending time with the addict to feel devalued in his eyes. As the addict continues to check his email and texts, he neglects his companion, who eventually realizes that he or she is a lower priority than the addict's phone.

Technology addiction also causes us to lose our empathy for others. We become less capable of understanding what they're experiencing. We lose our ability to sympathize with them. It follows that we become less able to grasp how our compulsive behaviors affect them. We develop a social blind spot. The blind spot makes it difficult for us to connect - or maintain connections - with others, including the people who are most important to us.

Erosion Of Interpersonal Skills

We assume technology improves our communication. And in many ways, it does.

For example, we're able to reach out to people whenever the mood strikes or need arises. We're able to connect with them whenever we want since most people carry their phones with them. If we need something from someone and don't feel like having a conversation, we can send a concise email or text.

But there's a dark side to this capability.

The more we engage online, the more our interpersonal skills deteriorate. The more we interact with our friends and loved ones through texts, emails, and social media, the more we dilute the real-world connections we share with them.

A lack of interpersonal skills poses social consequences. First, it impairs communication. Second, it makes one less inclined to listen to others, a vital tool for making personal connections. Consequently, an individual with poor interpersonal skills is likely to struggle in group settings and circumstances involving teams.

An erosion of interpersonal skills is one of the many ways a technology addiction erects a social barrier around the addict. The effect is significant. The stronger the barrier, the more isolated the addict will feel, setting the stage for anxiety, loneliness, and depression.

Chapter 5: Digital addiction

Most people no longer live their lives without smartphones. Thanks to modern gadgets, we are constantly in touch and up to date with all the news.

Digital addiction

But the flip side of this convenience is that we develop a pathological dependence on constant push messages, beeps, calls, and vibrations. We can no longer ignore emails, texts, and images.

Scientists from the University of San Francisco, Eric Peper, and Richard Harvey, in their study, published in the journal NeuroRegulation, argue that excessive use of smartphones gives rise to the same psychological and neurological mechanisms of addiction as substance abuse.

"Behavioral dependence on smartphones forms neurological connections in the brain in much the same way as regular use of opiates," Peper says.

The situation is aggravated by the fact that digital dependence has a very negative impact on social relations.

Studying the digital behavior of 135 students from San Francisco, Peper and Harvey found that those who spent the most time in front of their gadget screens felt particularly lonely, isolated, and anxious at the same time.

According to the authors, these feelings are due to the replacement of direct social interaction with virtual communication in social networks, which does not transmit gestures, facial expressions, and other non-verbal information.

Scientists also found that through an irresistible habit of distracting themselves with their smartphones, it was very difficult for students to concentrate while studying, watching other media, or eating.

In addition, dependence on digital devices did not leave time for the body and mind to recover and relax.

The consequence of this is the so-called "semi-tasking" – a situation where a person tries to perform many tasks at the same time, **but none of them are completed or successful.**

Pepper and Harvey argue that the responsibility for digital dependence relies on people as much as on the technical industry, which in its quest to get more and more profit purposefully uses the weak points of the human psyche.

"More views and more clicks mean more money," Peper says. Push-technology, signals, and alerts make us feel addicted because they activate the same nervous connections that in ancient times warned us about the danger, for example, the attack of a tiger or another large predator.

"Those neuropsychic mechanisms that once saved our lives now abduct our time, because trivial pieces of information activate them," the scientist adds.

However, there is a way out. In the same way that we can force ourselves to consume less sugar, you can make an effort over yourself and stop being dependent on phones and computers.

To do this, firstly, it should be recognized that technology companies manipulate our hazard reactions. Peper suggests turning off the functions of push, responding to emails and messages on social networks only at a certain time, **and set periods for work, communication, or important matters without interrupting the phone.**

Two of Peper's students have tried to change their habits of using digital technology fundamentally. One of them, Khari McKendell, six months ago, deleted all his social media accounts in order to build stronger social connections with people. "I still call and write messages, but I want to make sure that I communicate with people most of the time, not via the Internet," he says.

Sierra Hinkle, walking the streets, stopped using headphones to concentrate on what was going on around her. When she meets with friends, the whole company puts the headphones in the center of the table, and the one who touches them first treats everyone with drinks.

"We need to become creative and use technology so that they develop our abilities, but do not tear us away from the experience and emotions we can get in real life," says Hinkle.

Chapter 6: Preparing for a Digital Detox

Nowadays, various off diets, living a super healthy lifestyle or freelancing for income have become very acceptable. Similarly, Digital detox has now become mainstream. In fact, it is very necessary for people whose work is directly connected to the Internet. The Webby Award's Tiffany Shlain and co-owner of the media platform Huffington Post Arianna Huffington regularly undergo this procedure. Like any diet, this procedure must be carried out correctly; otherwise, there will be no result.

Many of us do not even notice how much time we waste on the Internet. The Internet seems to be a useful invention, but most of us do not use the benefits of the Internet, but simply waste our time.

How much of your working time is spent reading social networks, meaninglessly surfing the Internet, and inspecting Instagram feed? Hardly any of us seriously ask this question.

Closed virtual connections; do not let go after work. As a result, gadgets and social media, instead of being assistants, become our masters partly, devouring, perhaps, the most irreplaceable resource – our time. And this is not counting the deterioration of memory, problems with concentration of attention, and the ability to live an interesting real, NON-virtual life.

Salvation from the digital matrix of Internet connections and return to reality can be accomplished with the help of the so-called digital detox, which will help to "reboot," increase efficiency, and overall awareness.

You should be free from the matrix

The basis of digital detox was laid in America in the mid-90s by the movement TV-Free America, whose main slogan was "liberation from the TV." Over the years, the movement has expanded, changed its name to Center for SCREEN-TIME, and became the founder of digital detox. Every year in May, more than 300 million people around the world turn off the TV and all other devices (mobile phones, laptops, and tablets) for a few days to spend time in real life: family, friends, and nature.

Actually, this is the meaning of digital detox: to find the willpower in you to press the switch off on all available gadgets and social networks, go back to yourself, clear the space inside your head and make all the necessary offline things that your hands never reach. All the basic principles of detox are very similar to a small retreat. Only now there is no need to go to Shambhala to achieve enlightenment and awareness – simply log out of all available social networks, stop viewing someone else's life on Instagram, and start living your own.

Researchers of digital detox say there are at least four reasons why it is useful for each of us to do it:

1. Increased levels concentration

2. Establishing relationships with oneself and the world

3. Increased awareness and productivity in the Present

4. Reboots the brain and changes perception

As the American Internet researcher Frances Booth notes, digital detox can give you the opportunity to return to your own rhythms of life, to establish a connection with yourself, but also open the way to new ideas and solutions that can finally take shape in the mind simply because it will not be focused on millions of open windows and unnecessary communications. "Why it happens? Probably, because thoughts can finally take shape and lead us to judgment, and not be interrupted by a mobile phone call or a message about the e-mail that came in," she writes.

Jay Rangaswami, the chief research consultant for Salesforce.com, connects information absorption and Internet surfing to the process of indiscriminate food absorption. After all, our brain eats not only nutrients and glucose but also new information, images, and emotions. Scientists-neurophysiologists proved the link between the formation of new neural connections (synapses) and the acquisition of new knowledge. The brain includes more than 100 trillion synapses. New neural connections in the brain are formed every time you remember something. That is when you learn something new, the structure of the brain changes, so our thinking is, in principle, very plastic.

A good example of the emergence of a stable neural connection is driving a car. At first, it is difficult for a beginner to adapt to the need to combine different operations at the same time: control the road, switch gears, press the pedals, and still steer. However, gradually, the movements are already brought to automatism, which is more than confirmation of the consolidation of driving skills as a stable neural connection in the head.

Digital detox gives you not only the opportunity to return to your own rhythms of life, to establish a connection with yourself, but also opens the way to new ideas and solutions.

In the case of social networks, such new neural connections are more likely to harm than to benefit. Therefore, in order to productively perform their duties, you need to be able to disconnect from the virtual world. Reading mail, putting "likes" on Facebook, and so on, not only eats our time but also lowers the overall work efficiency, says Francis Booth. This information fast food not only expends our time but also eats brain space. The latter can be compared with a computer, where the function of the desktop is performed by our consciousness, and the subconscious is the hard disk. The more open windows in your browser communicating with the world around you, the more your system "hangs," the more energy your brain spends, and therefore, you in order to maintain optionally a million links, applications, and windows you don't need.

Therefore, the purpose of digital detox is the ability to close all windows in your head and reboot the system. The result will be new ideas, a surge of vital energy, the ability to control your time, good sleep, and the feeling that life does not end when your smartphone suddenly has a low battery.

Reading mail, putting "likes" on Facebook and so on not only eats up our time but also lowers overall work efficiency

Log off

By the digital diet or digital detox, you should be carefully prepared. Preparation can be divided into 4 phases, so to speak, four simple steps to implement "clearing the mind" of sticky Internet connections.

Step one is to remember your motivation, why you are doing it, what is your WHY?

Step two is to plan a detox as part of your social life. The ideal time to stay offline is at least 24 hours; the time can be extended up to 72 hours. It is best to carry out "cleansing" on holidays and weekends. Be sure to chart yourself what you will do during your detox, think up a plan: spend this time with those who are dear to you. After all, be in nature, a proven way to regain concentration. To get rid of the fear that "the world will collapse while you are away," warn all loved ones that you are planning to go offline.

Step three - after the world is warned, it remains only to exit from all social networks and turn off gadgets. I hope everyone understands that after turning off gadgets, almost immediately, there will be an irresistible, breaking desire to check mail or call. A feeling of anxiety will appear. This is especially true for those people who are used to being always in touch and instantly reacting to any requests from the network. For your detox to take place, you need to pull yourself together and endure this state. Important! Returning to digital reality can be painful because of the avalanche of information that has collapsed.

Step four is Logging in again

Users of smartphones based on Android are offered a more radical way to go through detox, a special application where you enter the time limit, and the system automatically blocks all incoming signals, such as calls, SMS, and mail. After launching the program until the end of the detox, nothing can be canceled. And this is perhaps the most effective tool that can be.

Chapter 7: How to Declutter your Life

Decluttering your mind must start with decluttering everything around you, and this means your space. That is the first step anyone should take. The process to clean and organize your things will help you make room in your mind for the things that really matter. Decluttering your home, your car, your desk – it is like therapy. By doing so, by going through all of your stuff, you will not only make some deep realizations about yourself, but you will see more clearly where your blocks really lay in life.

This process of decluttering is the first step towards taking responsibility for your life and getting your hands dirty. Sometimes we think we know where our negative thoughts come from, but during this process, we become conscious of things that were blocked in our minds. These are things that were forgotten for a long time but still haven't really healed in our minds. I believe decluttering your living space is the first step towards a more minimalist mindset. A big plus of this process is that you get rid of your useless things. It is also a way to liberate more time for yourself and for your day-to-day life.

Start with small projects

Of course, you don't have to do it all at once. On the contrary, decluttering will teach you how to be more patient and more disciplined in your life. So, you can start little, especially if you tend to accumulate a lot. Don't be too hard on yourself. Identify certain spaces in your home or at the office that could be decluttered quickly. It could be your bathroom drawer or your bedroom nightstand. It could be the closet where you toss all your cables and electrical wares (I'm sure everyone has one of those). We usually tend to accumulate things in certain areas more than others. Starting small with an easy project will give you the momentum to pursue your decluttering and get rid of your useless stuff progressively.

It can be a vast process, and you might find it difficult to know where to start and the steps you'll need to go through to sort everything out. That's why it's so important to start with an easy project first. When you begin to make room in your space, you'll start to feel energized and enthusiastic almost immediately. Decluttering can be a funny process. For some people, it might be really exciting and exhilarating when they begin to get rid of their stuff. It can provide you a sense of control and freedom over your life rather instantly.

Take your time with big ones

First, think about what you want the result of this process to be. How does this reflect on your personality and who you are without the noise, without the stress, and without the limitations of time? You will discover yourself during your decluttering process and this will be the time to progress onto the bigger projects. As Marie Kondo explains [1], taking everything out of your closet spaces will help you understand the real weight of your stuff on your life. That's why it's important to take your time during this decluttering phases in order to deeply understand what you tend to accumulate and why. These realizations will free you, transform you, and help you understand yourself at a deeper level.

For example, for many people, one of the biggest challenges during decluttering is when it comes to their wardrobe. Removing everything out of your closet and putting it on your bed is a good way to sort everything out before putting some clothes back into your closet. With this process, you'll immediately feel what it's like to have an empty closet, and it's such an amazing feeling! Then, you can put back your favorite items and get rid of the rest in order to only keep the essentials, and the important pieces that you feel correspond to your own style and being.

Other big projects could involve cleaning your kitchen and pantry. You can have fun with this. You can find new ways to organize everything that will make it easier for you on a day-to-day basis. You can also identify areas where you're missing important things.

Another thing you could try is to buy clever appliances online that will help you organize your stuff in a more practical way. There are a lot of very clever items to help you out, especially on Amazon. You can find beautiful compartments for your kitchen, smart hangers for your closet, and so on. Remember that you are a minimalist now. So, do not misuse your cash on cheap and useless items. Think about the long-term, quality materials when purchasing and the items that you will really need.

Blocks and struggles that you might have

There are some projects that you may find more difficult to start. You may have similar struggles with what we call your "sentimental clutter." These are the relics from the past; the emotional items that make you travel back in time when you pull them out to look at them. These are often gifts from people you love but, realistically, you never use or have items of a similar nature. And in a way, I think it's beautiful that these items can make us feel a flow of emotions and nostalgia. But if we really think about it, it's not so much the things but the memories we attach to them that make us feel this way. Don't you feel the same emotions when you look at photos?

Exactly..

When I find it difficult to get rid of this emotional stuff, I just take a picture of the item so I can remember it forever. Then I pack it up carefully and just trash it (with dignity). Or you can donate it if the items are in good shape or of value. Maybe it can be useful to somebody else. The important thing is that you keep in mind that these things are just things, not the memories themselves. All of the good and bad memories are still with you, in your mind, and you can access them whenever you want to or you need to. That is your power here, and with it comes the confirmation that you don't need clutter in your life to remind you of something.

Bottom line – Liberate yourself from your physical clutter to access a clearer mind, free from the past and free to move forward.

How distractions pollute our thoughts

Too many distractions will clog your mind emotionally.

Distractions are everywhere. To name a few of the obvious distractions we have TV, Netflix, and the Internet. It's like everything is designed for our passive enjoyment, preferably from the comfort of our couch. Even if there is nothing wrong with these activities fundamentally, you will discover that they were not only taking up a lot of your time, but also preventing you from having more energy, more enthusiasm, and more focus. I'm sure you know this too, even if it's difficult to recognize the fact that we spend too much time on these activities. And also, because it's difficult to change, isn't it?

But decluttering your space can't be enough to clear your mind; you also need to declutter your time. Life is short, and you need to take action if you want to find focus and peace of mind.

The goal here is to find out where your time disappears and where you can declutter. All of us at least have the same amount of time in a day whether we are millionaires, CEOs, or geniuses. Everyone is completely equal to this simple fact. All of us have 24 hours on a daily basis to do what we want to do in our life. And if you're reading this, my bet is that you may not spend 100% of your day doing what you're meant to be doing, right? But no worries, awareness is always the first step towards progress and the important thing here is to become more conscious of yourself so that you can declutter gradually of the things that no longer serve you.

Small distractions are often what is keeping you from accomplishing the big things. Multitasking is really a myth. Studies have proven this over and over again. Doing many things at the same time doesn't help with concentration and, in the end, it doesn't provide the same kind of results. So, how can you concentrate on one thing at a time? How can you ignore every single distraction of every typical day? Have you heard of the Pomodoro technique? It's a really simple concept to help you focus at work and get more things done. The technique consists of concentrating on one task for a limited period of time: 25-minutes. Use a timer to monitor this time and avoid other distractions while working during this time. This way, the running of time gives you a sense of urgency, enabling you to focus more deeply on that amount of time. Between the phases of concentration, you can have 10-minute breaks to help you keep a natural rhythm.

New activities, new you.

Your habits make you who you are. So, if you want to change your life and change your mind, then you'll probably need to transform your habits completely. Making room for new habits is the first step. And this fresh, clean slate will allow you to add different and great activities that will feed your mind with positive and efficient thoughts. What is it that you have always wanted to try and never had the time to? Which activities are you secretly thinking about in the back of your mind? Is it singing or writing? It doesn't really matter, because you're free to do anything. And maybe if you finally try it, you won't like it, but so what? There is also a good chance you'll love it. So, trying new things is never a waste of time, and, in the end, you may find something you're passionate about, something you truly love. You'll also like the process of doing it on a very consistent basis, even when it's hard or inconvenient to do. You'll love it anyway. I can't advise you enough to find what it is that you love to do, so don't be afraid to try. You really have nothing to lose.

Maybe you know exactly which activities you'd like to invest yourself and your time into. But somehow you never found the time to act on it consistently. In this case, you need to define some goals. Nothing can be achieved without a real goal, a purpose, a mission, or a vision. Find what it is for yourself and define every step you need to take in order to reach it. Say that you always wanted to learn a foreign language. What does it really mean for you? How can you act on this goal every day, consistently? Maybe you could organize a training plan with lessons, live discussions with a coach, or, even better, a trip? Anyway, put it in your calendar so you can actively progress on it and achieve what you want. You need a vision if you want to focus on your life.

Bottom line is free yourself from distractions and from what consumes your time to find more freedom to do what you are meant to do.

Chapter 8: Minimalism as a Position In Life

Minimalism is a way of life that helps people think about what or who adds real value to their lives.

This is a cleaning up of life disorder, which makes room for the most important aspects of life: health, relationships, growth, goals, and the desired contribution to this world.

It is necessary to understand that minimalism for everyone is their own and for a 50-year-old housewife, and for a 20-year-old novice startup starter – and this is their value.

Modern culture focuses on more since it is in our minds that we should strive for more. Minimalism is, we can say, the movement in the direction of "less." Pro ownership only that we really need and value. And not what is imposed on us by culture, society, and manufacturers.

Minimalism is not just about yourself. If "sustainable development" is not an empty place for you, then most likely, you are already minimalist in your heart. The planet is not rubber, and every person cannot own an infinite number of things. If the American level of consumption were established on the entire planet, we would not have stretched for decades.

The most minimalist countries are in Africa. But here lies the terrible truth: they are minimalists by coercion, and not by choice. What happens when their standard of living begins to improve? The same thing that happened in Western cultures.

How minimalism improves life

Mark Zuckerberg is a staunch minimalist. Not only him, but also other entrepreneurs, have repeatedly stated that they strive to minimize the adoption of insignificant decisions in their lives to the maximum. These people deliberately remove the excess from their lives.

1) Ownership, consumption, and finance

As a matter of fact, you succumb to the temptation and buy something not needed. Physical, or not, it does not matter: clothes, a bunch of incomprehensible accessories, a million subscriptions, or just a balcony full of junk. All this subconsciously puts pressure on your brain. Remember that feeling of freedom after you have removed something, washed the dishes, or raked your email?

But one cleaning does not get off. It is all in the system: if you once get rid of things, but do not change habits, after a while, you have to figure it all out again.

What about finances? There is an equation: earn more than you spend and keep the difference. But do not chase after income if you do not follow the expenses because you will still not be enough as a result.

Disassemble all your things with the question: "Do I need it, or can I get by/ask/rent out without any problems." Put a box with a "?" somewhere. Throw in things that you are not sure about. If you do not remember them for 3 months, then you should get rid of them.

If you have a lot of printed documents, photos, papers, scan, and upload to the cloud. But do not get carried away so as not to lose anything important.

Take a habit with each new purchase to ask yourself the question: "Is it necessary for me, or will I manage without any problems?" This should be at the level of reflexes. If you have difficulties with this, then try to sleep with this solution. Although we are irrational, we still have logic, and it should be used in an amicable way.

Determine for yourself the lists of desired and the limits of purchases of a certain category (clothing, alcohol, or sweets). This is a good limit. You understand what you want or need, and do not make impulse purchases.

Keep track of your finances. Why are companies watching the their costs, but people do not? In the 21st century, data is very much appreciated, and even more valuable is the information that can be obtained from them. Now there are many services and applications where you can attach cards and then analyze the statistics.

2). Mental freedom guarantees health

There is a direct correlation between external actions and what is happening in your head. Without learning to live consciously, a clean apartment will not help. But the opposite is also true: things will start to take away more and more energy and thoughts from you, putting you in a routine.

This is not only about the here and now, but also about the future that you plan so that it does not plan for you.

Well, it's about a "healthy mind in a healthy body."

- Get enough sleep. Just read this book for evidence.
- Start meditating. This will help you to become more balanced.
- Do morning exercises. You can experiment and add elements of yoga.
- Exercise 2-3 times a week. You should run/swim/ bike/lift/etc.
- Systematize life. Read this book or any book on self-realization and self-organization.
- Manage your habits.

- Do not focus on the opinions of others. But at the same time, "stay human."

3). Nutrition and proper diet

Food is the fuel your body works on. It is nutrition that largely determines the metamorphosis of the body.

Do not go on a diet or overeat.

Determine 5-10 variations of possible dishes that you coordinate when cooking. It can be different combinations of similar items. Simplify your eating, make all your meals in one day for the week.

And how do you apply it in business?

Fortunately, we can project our experience from one subject to another. What I want to say: if you began to simplify your personal life, then almost immediately, you will see a reflection of the results in your business.

The cleaner and more conscious of your life you are, the easier it is to communicate with you. Both partners and subordinates will notice this. If you have a significant other or another close person, believe me, they will see the differences first.

Chapter 9: Minimalism for your Health, Fitness, Sleep Routine and Habits

Your health, eating habits, sleep routine and fitness related activities play quite an important role in your life. A sedentary lifestyle, one wherein you are not active at all and you eat processed foods, you are likely to suffer from health issues. While this is not beneficial for you, a super active lifestyle, one wherein you exercise more than you eat and you starve yourself just to lose weight is not a healthy approach to live as well.

Minimalism advocates adopting a balanced approach to everything, which then enables you to enjoy that activity, benefit from it, but also keep it easy on yourself. Here is how you can bring in minimalism to your food, nutrition, sleep and exercise related activities and routines.

Food and Nutrition

- Slowly cut back on your consumption of processed and junk foods as they are saturated with trans-fats, genetically modified organisms (GMOs), processed and artificial sugars, salt and other ingredients, which are only harmful for your body and mind, and steer you towards high blood pressure, diabetes and other health problems.

- Add more whole foods such as whole grains and cereals to your diet.

- Incorporate fresh fruits and vegetables, nuts, seeds, lean meat cuts and organic products to your diet. Make that transition slowly by replacing one processed or junk food item with one healthy item.

- Try to cook meals yourself to enjoy healthy, home cooked meals.

- Only buy food when you truly need it and do not buy one months' grocery in advance as oftentimes, you tend to overestimate the amount of items you need, buy more and end up wasting up most of the purchased items.

- Prepare a list of all the food items you need before going for grocery and stick to it only.

- When cooking food, do not add too many ingredients, spices and condiments. Stick to a few ingredients and spices to enjoy their full flavor.

- Ensure that you have a healthy breakfast 30 to 60 minutes after waking up and space out the meals in a day about 2 to 4 hours apart from each other.

- Instead of having 3 heavy meals, it is better to have 5 to 6 small portioned ones so you stay fuller throughout the day and do not overeat in one go.

- Stay hydrated by drinking 2 to 3 liters of water throughout the day. This helps your body and mind function optimally, and keeps you from eating too much. Oftentimes, it is not real hunger, but being dehydrated that makes you feel you are hungry. If you drink enough water, you will curb unnecessary cravings and eat only when you need to.

- Try to avoid munching snacks every now and then. Often that happens when you experience fake hunger, which can be due to dehydration, boredom and the habit of eating all the time. If you feel hungry, but you just ate a nice meal an hour ago, ask yourself if it is real hunger. Distract yourself by doing some chore and if it is fake hunger, it is likely not to bother you again.

Exercise and Fitness

- Exercising is extremely important for you, as it improves the production of mood enhancing hormones such as dopamine and serotonin that boost your enthusiasm, confidence and emotional wellbeing. To enjoy that, incorporate a nice physical activity in your life. You could jog, swim, do Pilates,

Yoga, play a sport or do anything physical for 30 to 60 minutes, or you could engage in 2 to 3 activities for 20 to 40 minutes each throughout the day. You must engage in at least one physical activity 3 to 6 times a week to keep yourself up and running.

- Do not go overboard when it comes to being physically active. If you play basketball for an hour daily, do not spend 2 hours in the gym as well; an hour's workout in the gym would be enough. Never over-exhaust your body as your muscles can only handle a certain amount of pressure and burden.

- If you work out for long hours, ensure you eat a very healthy diet rich in protein, carbs and good fat accordingly and give your body at least 9 hours of rest daily. If you work out extensively, but do not sleep well and have a restricted diet, you are likely to damage your liver and heart.

- Do not go for an hour-long exercise or physical activity right away if you have not been active in years. Take it slowly and easy, and begin with just 10 minutes of physical activity. You could start with walking then move to jogging and slowly add in other exercises in your routine.

- Stay active throughout the day by walking more and when needed instead of sitting on the couch all the time. If your work involves a lot of sitting, get up after every one hour of work and walk around, stretch or do a few exercises such as squats and jumping jacks for 5 to 10 minutes at least.

- Take the stairs instead of the elevator when you can.

- Do your chores yourself instead of asking others to do them for you to become more active.

Sleep

- If you are not sleeping enough, you are certainly not doing yourself any favor. Your body yearns for sleep as much as it requires food to stay active and healthy. Analyze your sleep routine and if you get less than 7 hours of sleep daily, start improving on this. On average, adults need 7 to 9 hours of sleep at night along with a 10 to 60 minute nap in the afternoon. You need to slowly start getting better sleep by reducing your usage of screens before your bedtime, setting a proper bedtime and wake-up time and sticking to them for a while.

- If sleeping for 7 to 8 hours consecutively does not suit you, try the 'segmented sleep' technique. This refers to sleeping for 3 to 4 hours consecutively, waking up to do some routine or even a couple of important chores for 2 to 3 hours and then going back to sleep for another round of 4 hours or a bit more. This is how our ancestors slept and it worked out fine for them. If you often wake up in the middle of the night after sleeping for a few hours, try this technique to know if it can work out for you.

- Do nap for a little bit in the afternoon as it rejuvenates you and prepares you for another round of work.

- Do not sleep too much as it makes you lethargic. If you get 7 to 8 hours of sleep daily at night and nap sometimes in the day as well, do not go greedy on sleeping and find ways to stay in the bed longer. This will only harm your productivity and steer you away from your goals.

Spirituality and Activities Related to it

Spirituality is quite an important aspect of our lives, but sadly, not many of us are aware of it and pay attention to our spiritual needs. This is another reason why we are unaware of our purpose and clear goals in life.

Spirituality is a relative term and means differently for everyone. Some people perceive it to be able to build a connection with a higher force in the world whereas some refer it to finding your mission and sense of purpose in life. It can mean the same or something different for you, but whatever it is, you must find it.

Unlocking your spirituality is the key to figuring out yourself better and discovering what real value and meaning means to you, and what you truly associate with it. You can do this by reflecting on your thoughts, through reading different types of scriptures and texts, and by meditating.

The simplest way to meditate is to sit comfortably with your eyes closed, breathe in your natural manner and just focus on your breath for a few minutes. It takes time and consistency to build this focus, but once you establish it, you then find it easy to pause your barrage of thoughts and concentrate on one thing at a time. This slowly helps you unlock your spirituality.

You should engage in any one activity on a daily or at least a weekly basis for an hour at least to become spiritual with time. However, while doing that, again do not overburden yourself and meditate or fast for hours. Often people associate spirituality with a complete abstinence to food and sex, which again is an unhealthy approach. Yes, there are yogis and meditation practitioners who have that level of commitment, but that comes with years of practice. Trying to quit everything that you feel is a luxury right now cold turkey will only backfire so go slow and easy.

To ensure you stay consistent with these practices, track your performance by maintaining journal entries related to these activities.

Your relationships and social activities are another important aspect of your life, which too, deserve to be treated with respect and minimalism. The next chapter teaches you how to do that.

Chapter 10: Apply Minimalism To Your Relationships, Social Life and Activities

Healthy, loving relationships, a thriving social life and being involved in activities that bring you contentment and value does make your life all the more better, but if integrated with minimalism. Here is how you can transform these areas and make them more meaningful with minimalism:

Relationships

Having too many relationships is not a sign of a happy, meaningful life; it is the quality of relationships that matter. If you are surrounded by relatives and even family members who keep pulling you down, control, manipulate you, and add any sort of toxicity in your life, it is best to distance yourself from them.

Figure out the important relationships in your life and then ponder on what you want from each of those. If you wish to have an intimate partner, what do you expect from him/ her so you can focus on those lines and find the right spouse. If, however, you are in a relationship with someone, but things are not taking the right direction, reflect on them right now so you can call it quits before tying the knot with the wrong person.

Once you are sure on the loved ones you wish to keep around, spend quality time with them, express your feelings to them, have meaningful get-togethers with them, meet them on special occasions and festivals, and give them presents if you want to. A present doesn't always have to be an expensive perfume, it can be something simple that they will appreciate.

Social Life

Time spent with good friends is certainly special, but only if they are actually supportive and positive. As important it is to have a social life, it is equally important to analyze the kind of people you spend your time with as we are the average of the 5 to 6 people we hang out the most with. If you are hanging out with demotivating people who haven't accomplished much in life, or those who live an extravagant life and somehow influence you to do the same, you will never be able to successfully pursue minimalism.

Cut back on your time spent with such influences by clearly communicating your concerns to them and making a conscious effort to replace them with more meaningful and inspiring people. You can easily find minimalism based groups on social media and get connected with some lovely minimalists.

Activities

You should have healthy and fun hobbies, and take part in leisure-based activities, but even those should be the ones that you actually wish to engage in. Stop doing activities because your boss wants you to, or because your partner is forcing you to. Figure out what you actually wish to do and add it to your daily routine.

Working along these lines will make you feel empowered because you will make decisions regarding what to do and who to meet, which will only improve your life.

Let us move to the next chapter to find out how minimalism can be applied to your financial life and career.

Chapter 11: Apply Minimalism To Your Financial Life, Work and Career

Work hard and smart are both important in your life, but even that should be done with minimalism to achieve more value and empowerment. Here is how minimalism can improve your financial life, work routine and professional life:

Finances

Your hard-earned money has the right to be used wisely and not just on everything, that catches your fancy. Also, if you aren't able to meet your basic expenses with your income even though you know you are being paid well, it clearly reflects on your extravagant behavior. Here are some ways to improve on that.

- Make a list of your basic expenses such as food, grocery, utility bills, medical and health expenses, accommodation and rent, conveyance related expenses, car maintenance and fuel if you own a car, clothes and social activities. Figure out which of these expenses is actually needed and which ones you can do away with.

- Slowly cut back on your less important expenses and ensure that you save at least $20 every week and slowly increase that amount to $100 per week.

- Invest your savings in a good savings plan and keep some amount in an emergency fund to deal with emergencies.

- Do not add to your expenses unless it is a dire need.

- Cut and throw all your credit cards because they only add to your debt.

- Take out only the exact amount of money you need for that time from your ATM because any extra amount that you withdraw is likely to end up being spent sooner than you think.

Work

You must have heard 'All work, but no play makes Jack a dull boy' right, and so it is true. While working hard is important, there are certain rules you need to obey in that aspect too so you make the most of it and do not exhaust yourself either.

- Set fixed working hours and do not work longer than that unless it is an emergency. However, if you are extremely career driven and that is what brings you meaning, it is all right to work long hours for some time.

- Try not to bring your work home and keep it restricted to your office area. If you work from home, set one spot for working and do not talk about your work after your work hours. This keeps you from feeling exhausted and nurturing any bitterness related to your work.

- Work as much as you need to. If your basic expenses amount to about $1000 and your job pays you around $2000, and you are happy with the work hours, do not work extra and save that amount. If you work provides you with only enough to meet your expenses, but you are happy with your current lifestyle and do not wish to push yourself harder, that is great too. You have to evaluate your needs, goals and how much work you need to do to fulfill them to choose a convenient work routine.

- Take breaks in between your difficult work related tasks to rejuvenate your body and mind, and work more efficiently.

- Try the 80/ 20 rule when working, which requires you to invest 20% of your time, effort and money in tasks, activities and areas that yield 80% results. Economist Vilfredo Pareto created this rule when he observed that 80% of income generated in the economy was by 20% industries. This applies to almost all areas of your life. Minimalism is not just about clearing out unnecessary stuff, but also focuses on reducing your unnecessary effort and achieve more with less time and effort, which is where the 80/20 rule comes in handy. In your work, determine the activities that contribute the most to your output and earning, and work on them first with your maximum effort. Work on the other less important tasks later.

Career

Your career is an incredibly significant aspect of your life, an area which if you don't feel connected to can make you lose interest in life and feel unaccomplished. If you aren't too pleased with your career so far, assess your feelings for it and figure out a career option that excites you. You can then begin looking for jobs in it, or if you have some funds, find ways to establish your start-up in the area. Until the time you pursue it, do not leave your current job or maybe switch to a less exhausting one.

Assets

It is great to have assets such as a house, land, real estate, car etc., but you do need to analyze whether or not locking your investment in these things adds value to your life. For instance, there are people who prefer traveling through Uber instead of buying their own car because it is an expensive purchase and requires a great deal of maintenance, which will only eat away on time and money. Similarly, there are minimalists who prefer not buying a house and instead use that money to travel and pursue their other important passions.

You need to rethink your aspirations associated with creating more assets and if you feel they do not really matter to you, convince yourself to think less about them, and invest your income more on activities that bring you meaning and happiness.

Remember that happiness comes from having a well-balanced life wherein all the different aspects that matter to you are addressed appropriately. If you follow a minimalist lifestyle as discussed in this book, you can achieve freedom and pure happiness.

Conclusion

I really hope that the information you read in this book helped you. And you could tame the most terrible monster – the Internet, and now it doesn't rule you, but you rule them.

The Internet is a wonderful but overcrowded place. If you do not use it wisely, you will find yourself "drowning".

And, ultimately, in this life, we have all the tools we need for convenience: alarm clocks for every taste and color, excellent modern voice recorders, lightweight and powerful cameras, compact notebooks for recordings, paperback books and electronic books with a screen that looks like a paper page, and so on and so forth. Looking at the assortment, we must admit that we love our smartphones so much not only because they replace an alarm clock or a voice recorder, but also because they tie us to themselves due to less obvious mechanisms. They are pleasant to the touch, beautiful, fragile, they easily adapt to our habits, and they are always new, and "very much ours" - filled with personal photos, records, dialogues, and addresses.

They are such because "supply creates the demand," and "demand creates a supply." This is not entirely about the development of technology, and not quite about the development of society. A lot of very attentive people listen to everything we say about ourselves and about communication. After all, they need us to make a purchase; we need to provide data. They will do everything to maintain our interest since interest is profit. Are we ready to change our lifestyle so much for someone else's profit? This, of course, is another matter.

Reference

https://blog.rescuetime.com/digital-minimalism/

https://www.calnewport.com/books/digital-minimalism/

https://medium.com/swlh/digital-minimalism-how-to-simplify-your-online-life-76b54838a877

Made in the USA
Coppell, TX
14 December 2019